STAND UP
if you love
THE B⚽SS

A collection of poems written in support
of the Lincoln City Football Club

with special tributes to the late
Keith Alexander and Richard Butcher

By a lifelong Imps fan
Geoffrey Piper

With a Foreword by
John Saxbee
Bishop of Lincoln 2001-2011

"To the memory of Keith and Richard
and the future success of the Club they served so well."

Text Copyright © Geoffrey Piper 2011. Profits from sales of this work to be applied for the benefit of Lincoln City Football Club.

Acknowledgments: The author would like to acknowledge the valuable support and advice he has received from the Directors and Staff of Lincoln City FC, and members of the Lincoln City Supporters Trust, whilst writing these poems. In particular he wishes to thank the Club for providing such excellent photographs. He also wishes to acknowledge the considerable debt he owes to Ian and Donald Nannestad, whose "Who's Who of Lincoln City" and "Official History" of the Club proved to be invaluable sources of reference, and to Grahame Lloyd, whose "One Hell of a Season" provided some essential background reading on the 2002-3 season. He is most grateful too to John Saxbee, Bishop of Lincoln from 2001 to 2011 and himself a keen football fan, for his very generous Foreword. Finally, he would like to thank Rob Bradley, the Chairman of Lincoln City from 2001 to 2005, not only for kindly reading, checking and commenting on the initial manuscript for this publication but also, on behalf of all Lincoln City supporters, for the pivotal role he played in rescuing and stabilising our club during one of the most difficult periods in its long history. Without him, and a few others, there might not now have been a Lincoln City Football Club.

First Published in 2011 by TUCANN*books*

ISBN 978-1-907516-17-7

Design © TUCANN*books* 2011

Produced by: TUCANNdesign&print, 19 High Street, Heighington, Lincoln LN4 1RG
Tel & Fax: 01522 790009
Website. www.tucann.co.uk

CONTENTS

FORE**WORD**
by the Rt Rev John Saxbee,
Bishop of Lincoln, 2001-2011

Unlike cricket, rugby and horse racing, football has not inspired much poetry. But it should, because it is about rhythms and patterns and passion, and that is what poetry is about as well.

In recent years, fans on the terraces have come up with some pretty clever verses, especially when it comes to questioning the parentage of the referee or the personal hygiene of the opposition supporters. But Geoffrey Piper, the Bard of the Bank, has taken his passion for Lincoln City to a whole new level with this collection of poems capturing the highs and lows, the joys and sorrows, the characters and controversies characterising the beautiful game.

He opens with the Imp high on his perch in Lincoln Cathedral and takes us through the history of the club including many exhilarating victories as well as some tearful defeats. Long-standing supporter Norman Foster, star performers such as double hat-trick hero Andy Graver and stand-out managers like Graham Taylor and the late lamented Keith Alexander all get poems to themselves. But at the heart of it all is the club itself carrying the hopes and heartaches of so many people over the years.

Welsh rugby has its hymns and arias, and English cricket has its barmy army ballads. Well now, thanks to Geoffrey Piper's wit and wisdom, Sincil Bank has its own collection of epic verse to cheer the Imps on their way back to the Football League – and even greater things beyond.

John Saxbee,
June 2011

Stand up if you love the boss

1 · THE LINCOLN IMP

Where better to start than with our oldest supporter...

I suppose I was really quite naughty,
A hooligan, you'd call me perhaps,
But I was feeling a little bit sporty
When the wind blew me into the apse.

I flew all over the Minster,
I'd have walked if I'd been a bit taller;
Then I found myself facing this spinster:
An angel I think they did call her.

The next thing I knew I was totally stoned
(Though I swear I had not touched a drop)
And for hundreds of years I silently moaned,
Till I heard of a stand called the Co-op.

I liked what I heard, and one evening did steal
Down the hill to cheer for the team;
They got me to act as the mascot for real,
Then I found it was only a dream.

But still they keep calling the team "The Imps",
So I'm prouder than ever before:
When no-one is looking, I slip down for a glimpse
And I smile whenever they score!

2 · FOOTBALL'S FIRST CITY

Formed in 1884 in the name Lincoln City, we were the first of many football clubs to adopt the title "City".

There were the Wanderers and the Villa,
There were the Rovers of renown;
There was Wednesday and Victoria,
And a team called Walsall Town.
There'd been a Forest and a County
For twenty years and more,
But no football team called City,
Until eighteen eighty-four.

That year, in Lincoln's Monson Arms,
Amidst some calls for unity,
Officials from three local teams
Agreed to merge as "City";
They entered for the FA Cup
But it took a few more years
Before another club turned up
Which played to "City" cheers.

So eat your hearts out, Hull and Stoke
And millionaires from Manchester;
You're copycats, like Cardiff, York,
And Coventry and Leicester;
Your teams play with a borrowed name,
You've stolen our identity,
For only Lincoln play the game
As football's true "First City"!

3 · FAN OF THE CENTURY

A tribute to a young Lincoln City supporter, Norman Foster, who celebrated his 90th birthday in 2011 and still comes regularly to Sincil Bank:-

Some of us think we can call ourselves a fan
If we've been to Sincil once or twice before;
While others may argue that none of us can
Till we've cheered the Imps for twenty years or more.
But I know a fan who really is great,
The best fan under the sun:
He's been coming to our matches since 1928,
A supporter if ever there was one.

Norman's been an Imp in ten decades,
Seven times he's seen Lincoln go up:
He's watched us beat Man U, and both the Owls and Blades,
And he was there at the Reebok for the Cup.
He queued for two hours for a play-off ticket
And went down to Cardiff with us all,
Yet he also saw Jock Dodds – "My word he could kick it!"
And he worshipped the great Allan Hall.

So, those of you who now are just starting out
On your journey supporting the City,
Who go to the games to sing and shout
And chant things that aren't very pretty,
You've a lot to learn about watching this game,
Unlike Norman, who deserves his own entry
In the all-time supporters' Hall of Fame,
As Lincoln's "Fan of the Century"!

4 · PART-TIME CHAMPIONS

In the second season after World War Two, the Imps won the Third Division North with a team consisting entirely of part-time footballers.

They had their peace-time ration books, and their wages from hard toil,
And they also had their freedom (that Hitler could not spoil):
"Essential work" they did each day, for just three pounds a week
But twice a week in winter, off early they would sneak.

They'd leave work those two afternoons to train hard for the game:
It was all they were allowed - folks were treated all the same;
But on Saturdays you should have seen the crowds that they would pull,
To watch them play against the likes of Rotherham or Hull.

Their football earned these fellows a mere five pounds a week,
But of all our champion City teams, this eleven were unique:
They played the game part-time but filled the terraces and stands:
A team of honest workers with loads of ardent fans.

Most other clubs by this time had several full-time pro's,
And how the Imps competed, heaven only knows:
But, under young Bill Anderson, they were always in the mix,
We had some proven stalwarts and he taught them all new tricks.

They played attractive football, so saw lots more fans come down:
By November, fifteen thousand saw the game with Mansfield Town;
The "sailor" Jimmy Hutchinson had acquired an eye for goal,
And soon the Imps were starring in a table-topping role.

Things didn't all go Lincoln's way but it soon became quite clear,
If we didn't win promotion we would certainly come near;
A defeat away at Rotherham would have seen our prospects dwindle,
But we won a famous victory with a goal from Willie Windle.

By this time just one match remained, v Hartlepool United,
Twenty thousand saw us win five-nil and all got so excited!
That night we were promoted, due reward for such great deeds -
And next season we were up against the Spurs, West Brom and Leeds!

Stand up if you love the boss

5 · GOING TO THE BANK
**A brief personal reminiscence of a small boy's first visit to Sincil Bank,
many years ago:-**

Across the stony Sincil drain,
'Twixt terraced houses washed with rain,
In cap and raincoat, clutching ten-bob note,
I skipped with Uncle Ted,
My rosette roaring red,
Towards the South Park Stand.

Beneath that stand we stood,
That ancient pile of wood,
I, four foot tall, pushed forward to the wall;
No fire drill lapsing,
Nor wall collapsing,
Then... by the grace of God.

And He, up the hill, has a glimpse
Of our free-scoring Imps:
Cathedral class, our halves provide the pass
Which lets our forwards in,
And so we win
The Third Division North.

6 · THAT PROLIFIC FORWARD LINE

Lincoln City won the Third Division North in 1951/2, scoring an astonishing 121 goals in the league that season. The five forwards - Harry Troops, Johnny Garvie, Andy Graver, Ernie Whittle and Roy Finch - each scored at least 14 goals, Graver reaching 36 for the season in only 35 appearances.

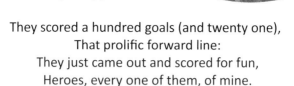

They scored a hundred goals (and twenty one),
That prolific forward line:
They just came out and scored for fun,
Heroes, every one of them, of mine.

Huge crowds turned out, week after week,
To see those idols that were mine!
Between their necks I strained to peek
At that fantastic forward line.

Some fine defenders played their part:
Jim Jones, Doug Graham, Horace Green,
Wright, Emery, Owen - skilful, smart -
But 'twas the forwards I had seen!

Somehow, some games we did not win:
How did we lose to Grimsby Town?
To fail at Mansfield, such a sin,
With forwards all of such renown!

But how the evening sun did shine,
When City did the title clinch,
With that amazing forward line:
Troops, Garvie, Graver, Whittle, Finch.

7 · DOUBLE HAT-TRICK HERO

Andy Graver scores six in the Imps' record-breaking victory over Crewe, in September 1951.

One day, in 1951,
One autumn afternoon,
We won a game 11-1,
I guess we were over the moon!

Eleven thousand at the Bank
To greet the men from Crewe,
But to tell the truth, and be perfectly frank,
The Alex just hadn't a clue!

Our Andy helped himself to six:
Two with each foot and two with his head;
Their young keeper, between the sticks,
Was making his debut, poor lad.

Our red and white stripes were rampant that day,
We really were in top gear;
We showed the railwaymen how to play,
Like we did to most teams that year.

A magnificent seven past Darlington
(Two weeks before Crewe got thrashed)
And seven more against Workington:
Goal after goal we smashed!

Those Imps could also defend quite well,
Jim Jones was a very good saver;
But the star of the show, the truth to tell,
Was Andy "Six Goal" Graver!

Stand up if you love the boss

8 · HEADY DAYS

Promotion to the old Second Division in 1952 brought the Imps face to face with some of the biggest clubs in the land.

In the Fifties, for nine seasons, we competed with some greats,
And we made some noise at Sincil, with near twenty thousand gates;
In John Charles and Johnny Haynes's league we witnessed stirring deeds:
We beat the likes of Everton and Liverpool and Leeds,
Trounced Leicester one day 7-1, and Blackburn once eight-nil,
All under shrewd Bill Anderson, some manager was Bill.

Poor Blackburn, in our first three games, allowed us fourteen goals,
Their team included England greats but for us these games were strolls:
In our first weeks in this league, with our promotion line-up still,
We beat the poor old Rovers twice, by 4-1 and two-nil.
Next season Graver netted four in the 8-0 scoring spree,
When we played them off the park with our forwards racing free.

It didn't matter where we went, or were facing famous names;
Liverpool's Anfield stadium saw some of our best games:
We went there in '55 and won comfortably 4-2,
Such victories began to be quite commonplace, 'tis true!
Five years later we returned and won again, this time 3-1:
Bert Linnecor scored a hat-trick, the Anfield Kop to stun.

We never made the top flight, that would have been a treat,
Though, in 1956, we were not far off that feat:
We had a midfield half-back line, which top clubs tried to steal,
Of Middleton and Emery and the dynamo Dick Neal;
But the whole of Lincoln's line-up deserved to share the praise:
For a modest club like ours, those were truly heady days!

Stand up if you love the boss

9. **THE GREAT ESCAPE**

Despite some spectacular results in those golden 1950s, Lincoln still had to battle hard most years to avoid relegation – never more so than in the last few games of the 1957/8 season.

Doom and gloom was all around
Our sad and sorry Sincil ground,
No smiling faces could be found:
Despair...

We hadn't won for fifteen weeks,
One of the very worst of streaks,
Our poor defence was full of leaks:
Dreadful...

Four points adrift by hot-cross-bun day,
We prayed in vain on Easter Sunday,
Six behind by Easter Monday:
Marooned...

But then we go and win a game,
And then another, just the same:
Less a flicker than a flame
Of hope...?

Two home games next, and quite a crowd,
Twelve thousand cheering really loud;
A spirit now that makes us proud:
And two more wins...

We've caught up now, but face a trip
To Huddersfield and must not slip
Else Notts and Swansea will us pip
To safety....

Harbertson scores early, stealing in like a ghost,
The Terriers, all over us, then hit the bar and post,
But somehow we hold on, and overcome the host
One-nil.

One game left - it had been abandoned in the snow:
We'd been three-nil down to Cardiff some seven weeks ago;
Then the weather intervened, so now we'd got another go:
Second chance...

The Welshmen returned on a Wednesday night in spring:
The excitement here in Lincoln did eighteen thousand bring:
Could we now escape, or was this our final fling?
Suspense...

I can hear the silence to this day, when Cardiff went one up:
They lobbed it over Downie and we thought the game was up;
Oh well, we'd had our run - we knew we'd not stay up;
But half an hour remained...

Then we crossed from the right, and Roy Chapman crashed it in;
And again, down the right, and Roy Chapman smashed it in;
Then Ron Harbertson let fly, and really lashed it in!
We've won 3-1!! And we're safe!!

We'd witnessed a miracle, like we'd all walked on the ocean!
We'd won all six we needed and there was utter jubilation;
We'd just avoided going down but it felt more like promotion:
Sensation... Elation... and Celebration!

10 · ANFIELD JOY

Lincoln City beat Liverpool 3-1 at Anfield in April 1960 - the Imps' fifth league win over the Merseyside club between 1955 and 1960.

There's a football team on Merseyside that plays in bright red shirts,
Which treats most of its opponents in a way that really hurts:
For more than fifty years they've been one of England's greatest sides,
Dozens of major titles, five European Cups besides.

But in the 1950s, despite stars like Billy Liddell,
They were in Division Two and playing second fiddle
To clubs like Lincoln City, who more than held their own
On their visits to the stadium where "You'll Never Walk Alone".

By 1960 the famous Reds had lost to us five times,
Including twice at Anfield, for them the worst of crimes:
They always thought they'd hammer us, but on the break we caught 'em,
'Twas we who'd hammered them, 4-2, at Sincil Bank that autumn.

Liverpool now needed a new manager, quite frankly,
And when we returned to Anfield, they had got one called Bill Shankly:
He greeted our Bill Anderson that day with a nice hot cup of tea,
"Enjoy this Bill" said Shankly, "for it's all you'll get from me!"

In his fifteen years as manager, Shanks got very little wrong,
But that afternoon he was up against a Lincoln team on song;
We sailed into the Mersey like a yacht with flying spinnaker
And completed a memorable double with a hat-trick from Bert Linnecor.

So, Lincoln fans, to those who ask what we have ever done,
You can tell them, for a start, we've been to Liverpool and won;
It may have been a while ago but Imps fans, man and boy,
Were on the Kop that April day to share their Anfield joy.

11 · THE BIG FREEZE

Thanks to one of the most severe winters on record, there was no football at Sincil Bank between Boxing Day 1962 and 6th March 1963.

One winter, in the sixties, in addition to the snows,
In Lincoln we had several weeks when every night it froze;
By March we hadn't had a game at home since Boxing Day,
In that time we played just two games, both of them away.

We were struggling in the League that year and the freeze-up made it worse,
The players couldn't really train, or set-piece drills rehearse,
For the manager Bill Anderson there was no respite from flak:
When we lost on the Pools Panel they said it's time he got the sack!

At least we had a "Cup run" that winter to enjoy,
We survived right through till March with a very clever ploy:
We were drawn at home to Coventry in F A Cup round three
But for weeks and weeks we couldn't play, for reasons all could see.

Day after day, from New Year right through till early Spring,
A fresh snow fall, or hard frost, would every morning bring;
Referees would make inspections but it was hopeless what they saw,
So "Lincoln City or Coventry" kept going in the draw!

But eventually, in March, a steady thaw set in,
And when we played the Sky Blues, five goals the Imps let in:
But by then we'd set a record, one for very chilly climes,
A cup-tie that had been postponed no less than fifteen times!

Stand up if you love the boss

12 · WEMBLEY 1966

There were at least two Imps fans in the crowd at Wembley
Stadium for the greatest day in the history of English football -
Saturday 30th July 1966 - when England defeated West Germany,
4-2 after extra time, to win the World Cup.

I watched with one who, orphaned by the War,
Cheered and jeered as if, hostilities resumed,
The men before us were the battle corps,
Pitted upon a poppy field and, all consumed,
To fight the fight and set the final score.

The bright green battleground beneath us lay,
Stretching to track and tunnel in the distance far,
The theatre for our epic play,
The scene for each new shining star
To claim his fame for ever and a day.

We strained each sinew with our troops in armour:
How we did urge them forward for the kill;
Ne'er had we witnessed such a panorama
Of shape and strategy and speed and skill,
Nor, for our ninety thousand, such compelling drama.

To and fro, and up and down, our nerves were torn
For two long hours, until that final burst
Wherein, with strangers on the lawn,
An immortality was gained by Hurst –
And national pride once more reborn.

13 · LEAGUE CUP FEVER

Sincil Bank's biggest ever crowd - 23,196 - saw Lincoln play Derby in the 1967/8 League Cup.

It may not have the glamour of the F A Cup itself,
But it's still a major trophy to put upon the shelf;
It's had several different sponsors, but in the early days
It was just the plain League Cup and not in the public gaze;
Some didn't think it mattered, something they would never rate,
But it was in this competition that we had our record gate.

By 1967, this League Cup was here to stay,
At last the top clubs showed that they were really keen to play:
The Imps had won at Mansfield and got a plum home draw,
A game against Newcastle, for some the first they saw;
When the Magpies took the lead our hopes did rather deaden,
But we equalised, then won it with a penalty from Peden.

Fifteen thousand came for that, on a fine September night,
Then a further thirteen thousand saw us Torquay disunite;
By this time we were in Round Four, which meant the last sixteen,
In a major national trophy 'twas the furthest we had been:
Twice in the F A Cup, in early days, we'd gone that far,
But never any further, so could this now be our year?

There was loads of interest now in who Lincoln next would draw,
It was mostly just the big clubs still competing in Round Four;
We were drawn at Brian Clough's Derby, a really daunting test,
But we rose to the occasion and played our very best;
John Kennedy and Ray Harford starred, and a goal from Lewis Thom
Gave the Imps a 1-1 draw and a replay back at home.

Stand up if you love the boss

So now the quarter-final draw included Lincoln City,
And out we came with Darlington, which some thought was a pity;
But maybe we could now beat both the Rams and then the Quakers,
Which, incredibly, would then to the Semi-Finals take us!
The next two weeks was manic and our ticket office buzzed,
We lost both our next two league games but were not especially fussed.

The League Cup, right now, was our main preoccupation
As we awaited our home replay with great anticipation;
Twenty-three thousand fans were at the Bank that night,
The place was really humming, torrential rain despite;
'Twas the Rams who took the honours and won the game three-nil,
But that crowd stood as our record - and I guess it always will!

14 · ARISE, SIR GRAHAM

Now for a tribute to Graham Taylor, the former Lincoln City and England boss, and arguably the Imps' most successful manager of all time

The youngest ever F. A. Coach,
Our youngest ever boss;
Now, though advancing years approach,
Still never at a loss.

Sixty years in the beautiful game
Since first he supported the Iron:
Along the way he's earned his fame,
From Imp to Hornet to Lion.

At Lincoln he moulded our best ever team,
A credit to club and community;
Of all our managers he reigns supreme,
Revered by all in the City.

When Elton took him to Vicarage Road,
Our luck we all of us cursed,
But, for the Hornets, the course he rode
Was from Fourth Division to First.

Stand up if you love the boss

On to the Villa - promotion again -
And League runners-up once more;
There was now no doubting his football brain:
You had only to look at the score.

As England manager, he lost only once
In all his first twenty-three games;
But still they said it was all long punts
And started calling him names.

Since then he's been the Wolves's boss,
And returned to Watford and Villa:
Wherever he's been, his departure's a loss,
His return a huge crowd-thriller.

Wherever he goes, to manage or play
Or comment, he knows not failure:
So when will we hear Her Majesty say
"Arise, Sir Graham Taylor"?

Stand up if you love the boss

15 · OUR GREATEST SEASON

As Lincoln City manager, Graham Taylor showed how a team's performance can be enhanced through an active involvement with, and in, the local community.   And how! The 1975/6 season saw the club breaking all sorts of records on the pitch, whilst also winning many new friends off it.

Graham had been boss for nearly three years
When we started this wonderful season:
And one thing was sure, we now had no fears,
For at least one very good reason.

The players trained hard, under Graham's regime,
Hard graft was one of his rules;
Another was that the whole of the team
Visit hospitals, factories and schools.

Ever since Graham had been in charge,
The club had been part of the City,
And the players were all made to feel, by and large,
They were part of the Lincoln identity.

So the people of Lincoln felt they knew the whole side,
And wished it to really succeed;
And the football team played with a real sense of pride,
Which was very important indeed.

Although they began with defeat at Newport,
They worked straightaway on their faults,
Each player took note of what he was taught,
And they soon got much better results.

By the turn of the year they were way out ahead,
With seventeen wins to their name;
And for the rest of the season, the table they led:
They expected to win every game.

And still they were out, all playing their part,
In helping the local community;
They also encouraged some new fans to start
Coming to watch Lincoln City.

The results kept on coming, the gates kept on growing,
Promotion was quite soon secured,
Over Easter, the Championship champagne was flowing:
Now the target was breaking the record.

This they did, for the Imps won thirty-two games
And lost only four all that season;
To this day there's many an Imps fan who claims
This was "City's Best Team", with good reason.

16 · CLEAN SHEETS

Another of the Imps' most popular managers adopted a more straightforward approach:-

There are many different ways for a team to succeed
At this mighty competitive game;
But as many a famous manager's said,
"To get a result" is their aim.
It's a simple game, they frequently say,
For all that you need to do
Is score more goals than the teams you play,
So it's best to concede very few.

The Imps had a team that played this way
Some thirty years ago, or more;
For the manager reasoned, both home and away,
We won't lose if the others don't score!
Colin Murphy, you see, had great foresight,
And argued that nobody beats
A team whose defence is really tight
And consistently keeps clean sheets!

Colin was our manager in 1981,
When we played in Division Four,
Many a game that season was won
By stopping the other team score;
We saw a new young keeper arrive:
A Welshman, called David Felgate;
With him we conceded just twenty-five
All season, which really was great.

We had Trevor Peake at the heart of defence,
And Hobson and Shipley up front,
So it soon became clear our tactics made sense
And we were in the promotion hunt;
We duly went up, thanks to Colin's foresight
And his theory - that nobody beats
A team whose defence is really tight
And consistently keeps clean sheets!

Stand up if you love the boss

17 · "WANT PROMOTION?"

**In 1982/3, with the Imps well-placed to return to the old Division Two, the
Board refuses Colin Murphy the money he needs to strengthen his squad.**

"Want Promotion ?", the leaflet said,
In letters that cried out loud;
"Want Promotion ?" the leaflet read,
That they handed out to the crowd.

"Want Promotion ?" : the players were tasked
With getting the points we needed;
"Want Promotion ?" the Manager asked,
But his words all went unheeded.

"Want Promotion ?" : they weren't being funny
When they called for the Chairman's head;
For when he refused the club any more money,
There were some who wanted him dead.

"Want Promotion ?" the fans all cried
In a crowd demonstration designed
To show they were all on the Manager's side:
And next week the whole Board resigned.

"Want Promotion ?" led to total implosion
As colleague fell out with colleague;
Five years later we won a promotion...
From the Conference back to the League!

Stand up if you love the boss

18 · STACEY AND WEST

Two lifelong Lincoln supporters, Bill Stacey and Jim West, were among the fifty-six people who tragically lost their lives when a fire broke out in a wooden stand at Valley Parade, during the game between Bradford City and Lincoln City in May 1985. Twenty-two years later, when the clubs next met in a League match on that ground, a short commemorative service took place before the game.

We did remember them:
Stalwart supporters of the Imps
Who'd gone as usual to the season's final game:
Their final game.

We stood in tribute twenty-two years on,
Paying respects before the game was played;
We tried in vain to sing "Walk on",
Lumps in the throats of all at the Parade.

We do remember them:
All fifty-six, including those two friends
Who give their names to one of Sincil's ends:
"The Stacey West".

We sit more safely now at all our games:
Fans housed in wooden stands no more;
Though it took till after all those Bradford flames
To change the law.

We will remember them,
Together we will honour them:
Bill Stacey and Jim West,
Now, with the will of God, at rest.

Stand up if you love the boss

19 · A DOG OF A DAY

In 1987, following a dramatic final day of the season, Lincoln City became the first team ever to be relegated (as opposed to elected) out of the Football League.

It was a lovely spring day in South Devon,
And exceedingly mild in East Lancs;
In South Wales the birds sang as though it was heaven:
A day to enjoy and give thanks.

But for Lincoln and Burnley, and also Torquay,
What mattered was who would survive;
To be fair to each club they all kicked off at three
So they'd finish together, by five.

At Turf Moor the Clarets were soon to score
But 'twas only a minor glitch:
For Torquay were losing at sunny Plainmoor
Where a stray dog ran onto the pitch...

We were struggling now against the Swans,
No songbirds for us in South Wales:
But we'd still escape the drop to the dungeons
So long as the Devon team fails.

It's five to five, and Burnley have won
While the Imps have been beaten two-nil,
But down at Torquay they've time added on,
They're playing dog stoppage time still.

Now we're waiting on news from South Devon,
And they score in the time they still play:
They've escaped, and their fans are in seventh heaven,
But for us it's a dog of a day.

20 · MURPHY'S MISSION

The club's relegation to the Vauxhall Conference in 1987 forced
the Board to make some critical decisions prior to the start of
the following season. The first, led by Chairman John Reames,
was to continue investing in a full-time professional squad.
The second, equally vital, was to lure the ever popular Colin
Murphy back to Lincoln for a further term as Team Manager.
The historic 1987/8 season was devoted to achieving "Murphy's
Mission", which was quite simply "Back to the League".

Under Colin we'd done it before:
The Imps had gone up a Division;
So before very long we all knew the score,
We were all right behind "Murphy's Mission".

The team went to places like Wealdstone and Bath:
We had to regain our position;
The club and the players all followed the path
Mapped out to achieve "Murphy's Mission".

With Sertori, McGinley, Matthewson, Batch,
Phil Brown and Paul Smith in addition:
All players of quality, surely we'd snatch
The points to secure "Murphy's Mission".

At Northwich we found ourselves two goals down,
No chance now to gain re-admission?
But we fought back to win, with a goal from Phil Brown;
We could start to believe "Murphy's Mission".

Stand up if you love the boss

With two games to go, we were one point behind
Rivals Barnet, who led the Division;
But they lost their next game and soon were resigned:
They'd lose out to the Imps' "Murphy's Mission".

Our final two games were in front of huge gates,
Drawn to Sincil by all the intrigue:
We played Stafford and Wycombe and, as history relates,
Won both and were "Back to the League"!

21 · BECK AND CALL

In October 1995, following the sacking of two managers in quick succession, John Beck became our next boss.

We 'd been playing pretty football without scoring any goals ,
We'd been dropping down the table and were really in a fix;
The Board had fired Sam Ellis and were in the worst of holes:
Could they sack another quite so soon, especially young Steve Wicks?

Steve had played at the top level with QPR and Chelsea,
And knew exactly what he wanted to help improve our team;
The trouble was we really needed quick results, or else he
Would have to go - our patience would soon run out of steam.

By October, just like Sam, Steve had got it in the neck
And the Board was holding interviews for yet another boss;
One candidate stood out - the "notorious" John Beck,
Who we knew we could rely on, to get rid of the dross.

Mr Beck came to Lincoln as a man of some repute:
At Cambridge he was known for his somewhat dubious tricks;
The corners were well watered, so chasing long balls could bear fruit
And the light bulbs, for away teams, they did never ever fix!

Whether this was true or not, under John we did improve,
We soon were off the bottom, with a very different side;
There was little "pretty football" now, nor many a clever move:
Just long throws, by Terry Fleming, to Ainsworth and Alcide!

With Barry Richardson in goal, most opponents we did tame
And gradually Beck turned us into candidates for promotion;
Then one day the police arrived, just before a match
And we saw the boss arrested, which created some commotion!

Eventually John Beck declared he never could be sacked,
He would remain as Lincoln's manager as long as he would choose:
"Oh really?" said our Chairman and Beck's bags were quite soon packed,
By now he was a manager we were quite content to lose!

22 · THE CHAIRMAN PICKS THE TEAM

The Chairman, John Reames, takes over managing the team himself.

One autumn day, when Lincoln were bottom of the table,
And yet another manager had recently been fired,
Our Chairman, Mr Reames, declared "I'm sure that I'm quite able
To manage team affairs myself - after all, I am retired!"

The club, when all this happened, was in Division Two,
And recently we had suffered defeat after defeat:
The Imps now clearly needed to try out something new:
In the past few weeks Man City were about the only team we'd beat!

So, for the remainder of the season, the Chairman picked the team:
One or two new faces and the odd old fading star;
He aimed to be "supremo", though we never reigned supreme,
Even when, as keeper, we signed Bruce Grobbelaar!

By this time Bruce had, long since, departed Liverpool
And couldn't help the Imps much, so he only played two games;
We picked up for a while and secured a victory at Blackpool,
But by now our hopes of staying up were going up in flames.

John Reames continued managing for only one more year;
(The Chairman had a word with him and said it's time he went!);
But he never gave up trying, the Imps to safety steer:
With his character and commitment he had something special lent.

He carried on as Chairman, our longest-serving ever,
Presiding through hard times when we looked like going bust;
And when his involvement with the Imps he finally did sever,
He kindly gave his shares to the club's Supporters Trust.

23 · GOING BUST

In May 2002, after years of difficulty with the club's finances, Lincoln City Football Club entered administration, thus becoming the first Football League club to be tipped over the edge by the collapse of ITV Digital.

For years the Imps had fought hard to survive,
At the foot of the Football League tree;
We just about managed to stay alive,
Thanks to sponsorship deals and TV.
As a club we'd always lived hand-to-mouth
Surviving from year to year;
We had no rich uncles like teams further south,
So we lived in perpetual fear.

As a new millennium and a new era dawned
We were promised an extra lifeline:
The Football League had a new TV deal spawned
Which was going to be a gold mine;
Clubs' shares were computed and budgets were set,
And this ITV Digital deal
Was just what we needed to pay off our debt
And stop our creditors making us squeal.

32   Stand up if you love the boss

Then suddenly ITV pulled the plug,
The Digital deal fell through:
For the Imps this was now a case of the rug
Being pulled just as payment fell due;
We survived, somehow, till the end of the season,
Owing money all over the place,
Before we went into admin, for the obvious reason
And desperately tried to save face.

The outlook was bleak, could the club still be saved?
We'd need hundreds of thousands quite quick;
The Board rose to the challenge, tough decisions were braved
As the candle burned down to the wick;
The manager went, and most of the team,
And we needed a miracle now;
Well, that's just what we got, in fact almost a dream,
Read on - and we'll tell you just how!

Stand up if you love the boss

24 · THE RESCUE

Under the Chairmanship of Rob Bradley, and with assistant manager Keith Alexander being put in charge of team affairs, Lincoln City lives to fight again.

It all looked pretty grim when the process first began,
We'd lost money all last season while we staved off relegation;
What we hoped for from the TV deal had now gone down the pan,
And so we had no option but to face administration.

This meant we had to cut our costs like we never had before:
We could not afford the manager, so Alan Buckley had to go;
The administrator made it clear we were now extremely poor
But we could keep Keith Alexander, on a budget very low.

The Chairman at this time was a supporter called Rob Bradley,
Who'd been persuaded to take over by the departing Mr Reames;
Rob was certainly an ardent fan, though not a rich one sadly,
Which meant we'd have to scrimp and save to put out decent teams.

Stand up if you love the boss

The supporters did their bit with the "Save the Imps" campaign,
Which raised a hundred thousand in lots of different ways:
The Co-op were fantastic, putting everything in train,
And the Echo helped, day after day, with each penny they could raise.

By August we could just about afford to raise a team,
Which big Keith had put together with some players from non-league;
To be at all competitive was a somewhat distant dream,
We'd just be pleased to hold on to our status in the League.

As most of us remember well, we not only managed that -
After nine momentous months we were chasing play-off glory:
When we got into the final, it felt like mortal combat
And it proved a step too far for us - but that's another story!

Stand up if you love the boss

SAVE THE IMPS, 2002
Caroline Strickland

25 · THE PAINTING

Not many Football League matches have become the subject of an oil
painting, but one of City's fixtures in 2002 was depicted on canvas by
the artist Caroline Strickland.   Shortly afterwards, with the Club now
in administration, the painting was re-produced in a set of numbered
prints, individually signed by the Club Chairman, Rob Bradley, and the
Manager, Keith Alexander, and sold as part of the "Save the Imps"
campaign to help raise much-needed funds.

She sat beside us, sketch pad held in hand,
Surveying all before her, all the while;
Distant from, yet near, the others in the stand;
The scene she studied for to suit the style.

The ground filled up - not very full, in truth -
Songs soon were heard from in the Stacey West
With lyrics that she might have thought uncouth...
But she was silent in her South Park nest.

The whistle blew and she did start to play
Her match with colours on her canvas fair;
Behind the goal, the great Cathedral grey:
A backcloth to the game beyond compare.

Sketching and shading she did never cease;
At times the crowd around her went berserk,
Then quiet again, and sudden peace
Descended on the ground and on her work.

Happy that day did Imps fans homeward go,
When at the 'death' we did a winner snatch;
But she had more than just three points to show...
For she'd produced a painting of that match.

26 · THE PLAY-OFFS

**Despite all the trauma of entering administration in 2002,
and the impact this had on the club's budgets, the Imps reached
the League Two promotion play-offs in each of the next five
seasons - sadly without quite being able to make that final leap
into League One.**

We all agreed we had no chance
After the pain of administration;
Even those who took a positive stance
Only thought we'd avoid relegation;
Big Keith had now been put in charge,
He would trawl the non-leagues and juggle;
He spent the close season searching at large,
But we still all expected to struggle.

Stand up if you love the boss

The new season dawned and we put out a team
With little if any experience;
We were out of our depth, or so it would seem:
For some 'twas their first league appearance;
The first ones to shine were a postman called Yeo
And a Tottenham reject named Gain,
A local boy joined them, the left-back Paul Mayo,
And we found our belief once again.

For forty-six matches they sweated and cursed,
They battled and struggled and fought,
There were no silly ego's, "Team Lincoln" came first:
Keith made sure they were all the right sort.
So we edged into the play-offs, against all expectation,
Where we beat Scunthorpe 5-3 and one-nil;
Suddenly Lincoln felt utter elation,
With flags draped from sill after sill.

For the final, we took fourteen thousand to Wales,
A day out, whatever it cost;
A day to remember, we all have our tales
Of a day that we loved, though we lost;
Our team had all gained some useful experience
Which would serve them all well for next year;
They all of them now had a big match appearance,
So we'd soon win promotion, no fear.

From then on Keith built the team slowly but surely,
The play-offs we reached every year;
We'd got Butcher and Futcher, McCombe and McAuley,
So when we lost there was cause for a tear;
We reached one more final, v Tilson's Southend,
Where we lost out in extra time;
On the play-offs for five years our fate did depend:
But we never quite crossed the line.

27 · "M" FOR THE MIGHTY IMPS

By the start of the 2005/6 season, the Imps were fielding a defence whose surnames nearly all began with the letter "M" - Alan "Mazza" Marriott, Gareth McAuley, Jamie McCombe, Paul Morgan and Paul Mayo!   Lee Beevers was the only intruder into this "M for Mighty" (and very effective) defence.

The Imps didn't often play poorly
In the days of McCombe and McAuley:
Our team rarely has a
Saver better than "Mazza",
While Morgan swept up very surely!

There was also Paul Mayo, and hence
We had a rock solid defence;
They gave us a glimpse
Of some real "Mighty Imps",
For that "M Team" was truly iMMense!

28 · THE WHISTLE-BLOWER
A gentle tongue-in-cheek "tribute" to some of the officials we have played against over the years...

Why is it that we always get a really shocking ref?
The ones we get are biased, as well as blind and deaf.
They're finicky on petty fouls, each little misdemeanour,
When, as everybody knows, our team could not be cleaner;
They stuff their little pockets with red and yellow cards
And dole them out for "fouls" they've seen from fully forty yards.
They just don't seem to see the dirty play of opposition
But, when it comes to our lot, it's a different proposition.
It's not that we resent it, or are feeling any rancour:
It's just that, every game we play, the referee's a... banker!

29 · THE TRUST IS A MUST

As Lincoln City (and many other clubs) have found, an active Supporters Trust enables ordinary fans to have a substantial stake in the club to which they belong.

The Imps were one of the very first clubs
To form a Supporters Trust;
Some fans think that it's not worth the subs,
Though without it we would have gone bust.

There are clubs who (whether they beg, steal or borrow)
Have budgets we'd die for at City:
They splash the cash like there's no tomorrow,
While we never have much in the kitty.

Sometimes these clubs are blessed with good luck
And find a good long-term investor;
But others just end up coming unstuck
And suffer like Boston or Chester.

The lucky ones have a good season or so,
They go up but, soon after, come down;
And then, when their owners get up and go,
They struggle like Halifax Town.

Having a trust is no guarantee
Of achieving success and stability:
It doesn't ensure that the Club is risk-free,
But it does help support Lincoln City.

So it's clear to me that the Trust is a must:
An essential part of the Club;
For fans to have a stake in it is only just,
And it's very well worth the sub.

Stand up if you love the boss

30 · A GOLDEN OPPORTUNITY

The Supporters Trust also offers Gold (and Silver and Bronze) membership, for those wishing to participate a little more actively. The Gold Members' scheme was introduced in 2001 and has raised well over £100,000 for the Club since then.

Imps fans, whether young or old,
All have the chance to discover Gold:
It is a metal you can trust,
Something of value which does not rust.
It's in the Boardroom, thrice a year,
And isn't really very dear:
We pay a sub – not very much
To meet the Board and keep in touch.

We meet on match days, around noon,
Though some can't wait and come too soon!
A chance to one another greet:
There's always some new friends to meet.
Very soon we get the call,
The Trust Chair kindly welcomes all:
We hear about the future plans –
More fun events for loyal fans!

And then the Chairman and Club Board
Tell us some things we don't record;
It's all quite frank but "Chatham" rules
Forbid us telling tales like fools.
Next the manager comes in
And tells us how he hopes to win:
He answers questions from us all,
For half an hour we're all in thrall.

Then lunch and tickets for the game:
Gold meeting games aren't quite the same -
We may be in a dreadful patch,
Yet somehow go and win this match!
But whether or not the Imps have won,
The day itself is always fun;
It's all to help support our team,
This wonderful Gold Members scheme!

Stand up if you love the boss

31 · WE'LL BE BACK

On 7th May 2011 Lincoln City lost its place in the Football League for the second time in 24 years (and the fifth time in its history), in front of a near-full house of frustrated fans. So what of the future for our beloved Club? The following lines were written, in philosophical mood, in the immediate aftermath of the Imps' latest exit from the League

These last few years have been utterly dismal
For Lincoln fans everywhere:
The team these days is just abysmal,
And now we're in the Blue Square ...

Almost eight thousand packed into the Bank,
It seemed strange to see it near full;
But all they saw was a ship that sank,
And they ended up going home tearful.

Some fans were angry behind the goal,
"Sack the Board", they shouted in rage;
But do we really want heads to roll?
We'd do no better ourselves, I would wage.

We've still got our Club, whoever it plays,
We're still here and no-one got killed:
We'll be on our way back again one of these days,
And then won't we all be thrilled?

32 · IF
(with apologies to Rudyard Kipling!)

If you can keep your faith when all about you
Are losing theirs and switching to Man U:
If you can trust your club when others rib you,
And smile whenever they are taunting you;
If you can wait for cup runs or promotion,
Sometimes for years and years and years,
But never make no trouble or commotion,
Nor blame the ref, nor shed too many tears.

If you can dream of winning Cup and League
(And if you can't dream, why support the Imps?!),
If you can meet both failure and fatigue,
And never mind when we are called the wimps;
If you can bear to see your favourite player
Transferred and coming back to haunt us,
Or ref's decisions which you think unfair,
Yet keep the faith whenever such things taunt us.

If you can celebrate the Club's successes
And share your joy with other loyal fans;
If you can cope with all the strains and stresses,
Whether the team are champions or also-rans;
If you can suffer the odd relegation,
And still support the club as best you can:
You will have shown true dedication
And – which is more – you'll be a Lincoln City fan!

Finally some tributes - and a fond farewell - to Keith Alexander and Richard Butcher, close friends who will never be forgotten by anybody associated with Lincoln City in recent years.
They were both much too young to die.

33 · RIP KEITH ALEXANDER...

Keith joined Lincoln City as a player in 1990 and, when appointed as our manager in May 1993, became the first black manager in full-time charge of a Football League club. He subsequently had spells in charge at Ilkeston and Northwich before returning to Lincoln in 2001, taking charge as first team manager in 2002. He remained in charge for the next four seasons, reaching the League Two play-offs every year. He subsequently managed Peterborough United and Macclesfield Town. Keith died in Lincoln on 2 March 2010 and the England team paid him their respects by wearing black armbands for their match against Egypt at Wembley the following night.

The gaffer? The big feller? The yellow socks?
How shall we all remember Keith?
Nay, how could we forget him? We were on the rocks
Until he gave us back our self-belief,
Restored our pride with four amazing seasons:
"Team Lincoln" he created with a shoe-string purse
And won our hearts for fourteen thousand reasons –
Alas, to suffer from that play-off curse.
"Stand up if you love the boss" we sang
In admiration of the man:
Our Sincil to the rafters rang
For he was loved by every fan.

He stood, head high, as does Example live:
A model for all who might to leadership aspire.
To all who'd seek for ways that they might give
And maybe help some youngster to inspire.
For never mind who'd won the game,
A friendly word to young and old:
A gentleman, he treated us the same –
We all belonged to one great family fold.
"Stand up if you love the boss" we sang
In admiration of the man:
Our Sincil to the rafters rang
For he was loved by every fan.

34 · AND "BUTCH"

Richard Butcher was born in Northampton on 22 January 1981 and was signed by Keith Alexander for Lincoln City in 2002, playing in midfield. For the next three seasons he played a central role as the Imps reached successive League Two play-offs, being on the field for every minute of our eight play-off games (including both our finals) during that period. He had two subsequent spells with the Imps and altogether made 123 appearances for the Club, scoring 12 goals. He later played – under Keith Alexander – for both Peterborough United and Macclesfield Town, scoring his final goal for Macclesfield only a few days before his sudden death, due to a rare heart abnormality, on 9 January 2011.

From box to box, from first minute to last,
You gave us skill and strategy and style:
The way you read the game, the way you passed,
You always played with craft and guile.

Three times the gaffer sent for you:
Here first, and then at Posh and Macc;
But you were Lincoln City, through and through,
How glad we always were to see you back.

And now we can't believe you too have left:
It's like big Keith has signed you up once more;
Family, friends and fans are all bereft,
But you're in the highest league for evermore.

Stand up if you love the boss